POETRY FROM CRESCENT MOON

William Shakespeare: *The Sonnets*
edited, with an introduction by Mark Tuley

William Shakespeare: *Complete Poems*
edited and introduced by Mark Tuley

Shakespeare: Love, Poetry and Magic in Shakespeare's Sonnets and Plays
by B.D. Barnacle

Elizabethan Sonnet Cycles
edited and introduced by Mark Tuley

Edmund Spenser: *Heavenly Love: Selected Poems*
selected and introduced by Teresa Page

Edmund Spenser: *Amoretti*
edited by Teresa Page

Robert Herrick: *Delight In Disorder: Selected Poems*
edited and introduced by M.K. Pace

Sir Thomas Wyatt: *Love For Love: Selected Poems*
selected and introduced by Louise Cooper

John Donne: *Air and Angels: Selected Poems*
selected and introduced by A.H. Ninham

D.H. Lawrence: *Being Alive: Selected Poems*
edited with an introduction by Margaret Elvy

D.H. Lawrence: Symbolic Landscapes
by Jane Foster

D.H. Lawrence: Infinite Sensual Violence
by M.K. Pace

Percy Bysshe Shelley: *Paradise of Golden Lights: Selected Poems*
selected and introduced by Charlotte Greene

Thomas Hardy: *Her Haunting Ground: Selected Poems*
edited, with an introduction by A.H. Ninham

Petrarch, Dante and the Troubadours: The Religion of Love and Poetry
by Cassidy Hughes

Dante: *Selections From the Vita Nuova*
translated by Thomas Okey

Arthur Rimbaud: *Selected Poems*
edited and translated by Andrew Jary

Arthur Rimbaud: *A Season in Hell*
edited and translated by Andrew Jary

Rimbaud: Arthur Rimbaud and the Magic of Poetry
by Jeremy Mark Robinson

Friedrich Hölderlin: *Hölderlin's Songs of Light: Selected Poems*
translated by Michael Hamburger

Rainer Maria Rilke: *Dance the Orange:* Selected Poems
translated by Michael Hamburger

Rilke: Space, Essence and Angels in the Poetry of Rainer Maria Rilke
by B.D. Barnacle

German Romantic Poetry: Goethe, Novalis, Heine, Hölderlin
by Carol Appleby

Arseny Tarkovsky: *Life, Life: Selected Poems*
translated by Virginia Rounding

Emily Dickinson: *Wild Nights: Selected Poems*
selected and introduced by Miriam Chalk

Cavafy: Anatomy of a Soul
by Matt Crispin

FRANCESCO PETRARCH

FIFTEEN SONNETS OF PETRARCH

FRANCESCO PETRARCH

FIFTEEN SONNETS OF PETRARCH

Selected and Translated
by Thomas Wentworth Higginson

Edited by Cassidy Hughes

CRESCENT MOON

CRESCENT MOON PUBLISHING
P.O. Box 1312, Maidstone
Kent, ME14 5XU
Great Britain
ww.crmoon.com

First published 1900/ 1903. This edition 2017.

Printed and bound in the U.S.A.
Set in Book Antiqua 10 on 14pt.
Designed by Radiance Graphics.

British Library Cataloguing in Publication data

ISBN-13 9781861715982

CONTENTS

A NOTE ON THE TEXT

The poems and translations are from Francesco Petrarch, *Fifteen Sonnets of Petrarch*, selected and translated by Thomas Wentworth Higginson, published by Houghton Mifflin & Company, Boston and New York, 1903.

Petrarch (below).
Manuscript by Petrarch
(left, found in 1985).

Marie Spartali Stillman, The First Meeting of Petrarch and Laura de Sade

INTRODUCTION[1]

BY THOMAS WENTWORTH HIGGINSON

Near my summer home there is a little cove or landing by the bay, where nothing larger than a boat can ever anchor. I sit above it now, upon the steep bank, knee-deep in buttercups, and amid grass so lush and green that it seems to ripple and flow instead of waving. Below lies a tiny beach, strewn with a few bits of driftwood and some purple shells, and so sheltered by projecting walls that its wavelets plash but lightly. A little farther out the sea breaks more roughly over submerged rocks, and the waves lift themselves, before breaking, in an indescribable way, as if each gave a glimpse through a translucent window, beyond which all ocean's depths might be clearly seen, could one but hit the proper angle of vision. On the right side of my retreat a high wall limits the view, while close upon the left the crumbling parapet of Fort Greene stands out into the foreground, its verdant scarp so relieved against the blue water that each inward bound schooner seems to sail into a cave of grass. In the middle distance is a white lighthouse, and beyond lie the round tower of old Fort Louis, and the soft low walls of Conanicut.

Behind me an oriole chirrups in triumph amid the birch-trees

---

1 NOTE: This introduction is based essentially upon a paper 'Sunshine and Petrarch' which originally included most of the sonnets in this volume. It was written at Newport, R.I., where the translator was then residing.

which wave around the house of the haunted window; before me a kingfisher pauses and waits, and a darting blackbird shows the scarlet on his wings. Sloops and schooners constantly come and go, careening in the wind, their white sails taking, if remote enough, a vague blue mantle from the delicate air. Sailboats glide in the distance, – each a mere white wing of canvas, – or coming nearer, and glancing suddenly into the cove, are put as suddenly on the other tack, and almost in an instant seem far away. There is to-day such a live sparkle on the water, such a luminous freshness on the grass, that it seems, as is often the case in early June, as if all history were a dream, and the whole earth were but the creation of a summer's day.

If Petrarch still knows and feels the consummate beauty of these earthly things, it may seem to him some repayment for the sorrows of a lifetime that one reader, after all this lapse of years, should choose his sonnets to match this grass, these blossoms, and the soft lapse of these blue waves. Yet any longer or more continuous poem would be out of place to-day. I fancy that this narrow cove prescribes the proper limits of a sonnet; and when I count the lines of ripple within yonder projecting wall, there proves to be room for just fourteen. Nature meets our whims with such little fitnesses. The words which build these delicate structures of Petrarch's are as soft and fine and close-textured as the sands upon this tiny beach, and their monotone, if such it be, is the monotone of the neighboring ocean. Is it not possible, by bringing such a book into the open air, to separate it from the grimness of commentators, and bring it back to life and light and Italy? The beautiful earth is the same as when this poetry and passion were new; there is the same sunlight, the same blue water and green grass; yonder pleasure-boat might bear, for aught we know, the friends and lovers of five centuries ago; Petrarch and Laura might be there, with Boccaccio and Fiammetta as comrades, and with Chaucer as their stranger guest. It bears, at any rate, if I know its voyagers, eyes as lustrous, voices as sweet. With the world thus young, beauty eternal, fancy free, why should these delicious Italian pages exist but to be tortured into grammatical examples?

Is there no reward to be imagined for a delightful book that can match Browning's fantastic burial of a tedious one? When it has sufficiently basked in sunshine, and been cooled in pure salt air, when it has bathed in heaped clover, and been scented, page by page, with melilot, cannot its beauty once more blossom, and its buried loves revive?

Emboldened by such influences, at least let me translate a sonnet (*Lieti fiori e felici*), and see if anything is left after the sweet Italian syllables are gone. Before this continent was discovered, before English literature existed, when Chaucer was a child these words were written. Yet they are to-day as fresh and perfect as these laburnum blossoms that droop above my head. And as the variable and uncertain air comes freighted with clover-scent from yonder field, so floats through these long centuries a breath of fragrance, the memory of Laura.

Goethe compared translators to carriers, who convey good wine to market, though it gets unaccountably watered by the way. The more one praises a poem, the more absurd becomes one's position, perhaps, in trying to translate it. If it is so admirable, – is the natural inquiry, – why not let it alone? It is a doubtful blessing to the human race, that the instinct of translation still prevails, stronger than reason; and after one has once yielded to it, then each untranslated favorite is like the trees round a backwoodsman's clearing, each of which stands, a silent defiance, until he has cut it down. Let us try the axe again. This is to Laura singing *Quando Amor*.

As I look across the bay, there is seen resting over all the hills, and even upon every distant sail, an enchanted veil of palest blue, that seems woven out of the very souls of happy days, – a bridal veil, with which the sunshine weds this soft landscape in summer. Such and so indescribable is the atmospheric film that hangs over these poems of Petrarch's; there is a delicate haze about the words, that vanishes when you touch them, and reappears as you recede. How it clings, for instance, round this sonnet, *Aura che quelle chiome*!

Consider also the pure and reverential tenderness of one like this, *Qual donna attende*). A companion sonnet, on the other hand, *O passi sparsi*, seems rather to be of the Shakespearean type; the successive phrases set sail, one by one, like a yacht squadron; each spreads its graceful wings and glides away. It is hard to handle this white canvas without soiling. Macgregor, in the only version of this sonnet which I have seen, abandons all attempt at rhyme; but to follow the strict order of the original in this respect is a part of the pleasant problem which one cannot bear to forgo. And there seems a kind of deity who presides over this union of languages, and who sometimes silently lays the words in order, after all one's poor attempts have failed.

Yonder flies a kingfisher, and pauses, fluttering like a butterfly in the air, then dives toward a fish, and, failing, perches on the projecting wall. Doves from neighboring dove-cots alight on the parapet of the fort, fearless of the quiet cattle who find there a breezy pasture. These doves, in taking flight, do not rise from the ground at once, but, edging themselves closer to the brink, with a caution almost ludicrous in such airy things, thrust themselves upon the breeze with a shy little hop, and at the next moment are securely on the wing.

How the abundant sunlight inundates everything! The great clumps of grass and clover are imbedded in it to the roots; it flows in among their stalks, like water; the lilac-bushes bask in it eagerly; the topmost leaves of the birches are burnished. A vessel sails by with plash and roar, and all the white spray along her side is sparkling with sunlight. Yet there is sorrow in the world, and it reached Petrarch even before Laura died, – when it reached her. One exquisite sonnet, *I' vidi in terra*, shows this to have been true.

These sonnets are in Petrarch's earlier manner; but the death of Laura brought a change. Look at yonder schooner coming down the bay straight toward us; she is hauled close to the wind, her jib is white in the sunlight, her larger sails are touched with the same snowy lustre, and all the swelling canvas is rounded into such lines of beauty as scarcely anything else in the world – hardly even the perfect outlines of the human form – can give. Now she comes up into the wind, and goes about with a strong flapping of her sails, smiting on the ear at a half-mile's distance; then she glides off on the other tack, showing the shadowed side of her sails, until she reaches the distant zone of haze. So change the sonnets after Laura's death, growing shadowy as they recede, until the very last, *Gli occhi di ch'io parlai,* seems to merge itself in the blue distance.

•

"And yet I live!" (*Ed io pur vivo*) What a pause is implied before these words with which the closing sestet of this sonnet begins! the drawing of a long breathy immeasurably long; like that vast interval of heart-beats which precedes Shakespeare's 'Since Cleopatra died.' I can think of no other passage in literature that has in it the same wide spaces of emotion. Another sonnet, *Soleasi nel mio cor,* which is still more retrospective, seems to me the most stately and concentrated in the whole volume. It is the sublimity of a despair not to be relieved by utterance. In a later strain, *Levommi il mio pensier,* he rises to that dream which is more than earth's realities.

It vindicates the emphatic reality and personality of Petrarch's love, after all, that when from these heights of vision he surveys and resurveys his life's long dream, it becomes to him more and more definite, as well as more poetic, and is farther and farther from a merely vague sentimentalism. In his later sonnets, Laura grows more distinctly individual to us; her traits show themselves as more characteristic, her temperament more intelligible, her precise influence upon Petrarch clearer. What delicate accuracy of delineation is seen, for instance, in the sonnet *Dolci durezze*! In the sonnet *Gli angeli eletti* visions multiply upon visions. Would that one could transfer into English the delicious way in which the sweet Italian rhymes recur and surround and seem to embrace each other, and are woven and unwoven and interwoven, like the heavenly hosts that gathered around Laura.

Petrarch's odes and sonnets are but parts of one symphony, leading us through a passion strengthened by years and only purified by death, until at last the graceful lay becomes an anthem and a 'Nunc dimittis.' In the closing sonnets Petrarch withdraws from the world, and they seem like voices from a cloister, growing more and more solemn till the door is closed. This is one of the last, *Dicemi spesso*. How true is its concluding line! Who can wonder that women prize beauty, and are intoxicated by their own fascinations, when these fragile gifts are yet strong enough to outlast all the memories of statesmanship and war? Next to the immortality of genius is that which genius may confer upon the object of its love. Laura, while she lived, was simply one of a hundred or a thousand beautiful and gracious Italian women; she had her loves and aversions, joys and griefs; she cared dutifully for her household, and embroidered the veil which Petrarch loved; her memory appeared as fleeting and unsubstantial as that of woven tissue. After five centuries we find that no armor of that iron age was so enduring. The kings whom she honored, the popes whom she revered are dust, and their memory is dust, but literature is still fragrant with her name. An impression which has endured so long is ineffaceable; it is an earthly immortality.

"Time is the chariot of all ages to carry men away, and beauty cannot bribe this charioteer." Thus wrote Petrarch in his Latin essays; but his love had wealth that proved resistless, and for Laura the chariot stayed.

FRANCESCO PETRARCH

TIMELINE[2]

1304.
Born at Arezzo, the 20th of July.

1305.
Is taken to Incisa at the age of seven months, where he remains seven years.

1312.
Is removed to Pisa, where he remains seven months.

1313.
Accompanies his parents to Avignon.

1315.
Goes to live at Carpentras.

1319.
Is sent to Montpellier.

---

2 Taken from Francesco Petrarch, *The Sonnets, Triumphs and Other Poems of Petrarch*, edited by Thomas Campbell, and published by George Bell & Sons, London, 1879.

1323.

Is removed to Bologna.

1326.

Returns to Avignon – loses his parents – contracts a friendship
with James Colonna.

1327.

Falls in love with Laura.

1330.

Goes to Lombes with James Colonna – forms acquaintance with
Socrates and Lælius – and returns to Avignon to live in the house
of Cardinal Colonna.

1331.

Travels to Paris – travels through Flanders and Brabant, and
visits a part of Germany.

1333.

His first journey to Rome – his long navigation as far as the
coast of England – his return to Avignon.

1337.

Birth of his son John – he retires to Vaucluse.

1339.

Commences writing his epic poem, "Africa."

1340.

Receives an invitation from Rome to come and be crowned as
Laureate – and another invitation, to the same effect, from Paris.

1341.

Goes to Naples, and thence to Rome, where he is crowned in

the Capitol – repairs to Parma – death of Tommaso da Messina and James Colonna.

1342.
Goes as orator of the Roman people to Clement VI. at Avignon – Studies the Greek language under Barlaamo.

1343.
Birth of his daughter Francesca – he writes his dialogues "De secreto conflictu curarum suarum" – is sent to Naples by Clement VI. and Cardinal Colonna – goes to Rome for a third and a fourth time – returns from Naples to Parma.

1344.
Continues to reside in Parma.

1345.
Leaves Parma, goes to Bologna, and thence to Verona – returns to Avignon.

1346.
Continues to live at Avignon – is elected canon of Parma.

1347.
Revolution at Rome – Petrarch's connection with the Tribune – takes his fifth journey to Italy – repairs to Parma.

1348.
Goes to Verona – death of Laura – he returns again to Parma – his autograph memorandum in the Milan copy of Virgil – visits Manfredi, Lord of Carpi, and James Carrara at Padua.

1349.
Goes from Parma to Mantua and Ferrara – returns to Padua, and receives, probably in this year, a canonicate in Padua.

1350.

Is raised to the Archdeaconry of Parma – writes to the Emperor Charles IV. – goes to Rome, and, in going and returning, stops at Florence.

1351.

Writes to Andrea Dandolo with a view to reconcile the Venetians and Florentines – the Florentines decree the restoration of his paternal property, and send John Boccaccio to recall him to his country – he returns, for the sixth time, to Avignon – is consulted by the four Cardinals, who had been deputed to reform the government of Rome.

1352.

Writes to Clement VI. the letter which excites against him the enmity of the medical tribe – begins writing his treatise "De Vita Solitaria."

1353.

Visits his brother in the Carthusian monastery of Monte Rivo – writes his treatise "De Otio Religiosorum" – returns to Italy – takes up his abode with the Visconti – is sent by the Archbishop Visconti to Venice, to negotiate a peace between the Venetians and Genoese.

1354.

Visits the Emperor at Mantua.

1355.

His embassy to the Emperor – publishes his "Invective against a Physician."

1360.

His embassy to John, King of France.

1361.

Leaves Milan and settles at Venice – gives his library to the Venetians.

1364.

Writes for Lucchino del Verme his treatise "De Officio et Virtutibus Imperatoris."

1366.

Writes to Urban V. imploring him to remove the Papal residence to Rome – finishes his treatise "De Remediis utriusque Fortunæ."

1368.

Quits Venice – four young Venetians, either in this year or the preceding, promulgate a critical judgment against Petrarch – repairs to Pavia to negotiate peace between the Pope's Legate and the Visconti.

1370.

Sets out to visit the Pontiff – is taken ill at Ferrara – retires to Arquà among the Euganean hills.

1371.

Writes his "Invectiva contra Gallum." and his "Epistle to Posterity."

1372.

Writes for Francesco da Carrara his essay "De Republica optime administranda."

1373.

Is sent to Venice by Francesco da Carrara.

1374.

Translates the Griseldis of Boccaccio – dies on the 18th of July in the same year.

SONNETS FROM
THE *CANZONIERE*

I

Lieti fiori e felici, e ben nate erbe,
Che Madonna, pensando, premer sole;
Piaggia ch'ascolti sue dolci parole,
E del bel piede alcun vestigio serbe;
Schietti arboscelli, e verdi frondi acerbe;
Amorosette e pallide viole;
Ombrose selve, ove percote il Sole,
Che vi fa co' suoi raggi alte e superbe;
O soave contrada, o puro fiume,
Che bagni 'l suo bel viso e gli occhi chiari,
E prendi qualità dal vivo lume;
Quanto v'invidio gli atti onesti e cari!
Non fia in voi scoglio omai che per costume
D'arder con la mia fiamma non impari.

(Sonnet 162)

I

O joyous, blossoming, ever-blessed flowers!
'Mid which my pensive queen her footstep sets;
O plain, that hold'st her words for amulets
And keep'st her footsteps in thy leafy bowers!
O trees, with earliest green of springtime hours,
And all spring's pale and tender violets!
O grove, so dark the proud sun only lets
His blithe rays gild the outskirts of thy towers!
O pleasant country-side! O limpid stream,
That mirrorest her sweet face, her eyes so clear,
And of their living light canst catch the beam!
I envy thee her presence pure and dear.
There is no rock so senseless but I deem
It burns with passion that to mine is near.

II

Quando Amor i begli occhi a terra inchina
E i vaghi spirti in un sospiro accoglie
Con le sue mani, e poi in voce gli scioglie
Chiara, soave, angelica, divina;
Sento far del mio cor dolce rapina,
E sì dentro cangiar pensieri e voglie,
Ch'i' dico: or fien di me l'ultime spoglie,
Se 'l Ciel sì onesta morte mi destina.
Ma 'l suon, che di dolcezza i sensi lega,
Col gran desir d'udendo esser beata,
L'anima, al dipartir presta, raffrena.
Così mi vivo, e così avvolge e spiega
Lo stame della vita che m'è data,
Questa sola fra noi del ciel sirena.

(Sonnet 167)

II

When Love doth those sweet eyes to earth incline,
And weaves those wandering notes into a sigh
With his own touch, and leads a minstrelsy
Clear-voiced and pure, angelic and divine, –
He makes sweet havoc in this heart of mine,
And to my thoughts brings transformation high,
So that I say, "My time has come to die,
If fate so blest a death for me design."
But to my soul, thus steeped in joy, the sound
Brings such a wish to keep that present heaven,
It holds my spirit back to earth as well.
And thus I live: and thus is loosed and wound
The thread of life which unto me was given
By this sole Siren who with us doth dwell.

III

Aura che quelle chiome bionde e crespe
Circondi e movi, e se' mossa da loro
Soavemente, e spargi quel dolce oro,
E poi 'l raccogli e 'n bei nodi 'l rincrespe;
Tu stai negli occhi ond'amorose vespe
Mi pungon sì, che 'nfin qua il sento e ploro;
E vacillando cerco il mio tesoro,
Com'animal che spesso adombre e 'ncespe:
Ch'or mel par ritrovar, ed or m'accorgo
Ch'i' ne son lunge; or mi sollevo, or caggio:
Ch'or quel ch'i' bramo, or quel ch'è vero, scorgo.
Aer felice, col bel vivo raggio
Rimanti. E tu, corrente e chiaro gorgo,
Ché non poss'io cangiar teco viaggio?

(Sonnet 227)

III

Sweet air, that circlest round those radiant tresses,
And floatest, mingled with them, fold on fold,
Deliciously, and scatterest that fine gold,
Then twinest it again, my heart's dear jesses;
Thou lingerest on those eyes, whose beauty presses
Stings in my heart that all its life exhaust,
Till I go wandering round my treasure lost,
Like some scared creature whom the night distresses.
I seem to find her now, and now perceive
How far away she is; now rise, now fall;
Now what I wish, now what is true, believe.
O happy air! since joys enrich thee all,
Rest thee; and thou, O stream too bright to grieve!
Why can I not float with thee at thy call?

IV

Qual donna attende a gloriosa fama
Di senno, di valor, di cortesia,
Miri fiso negli occhi a quella mia
Nemica, che mia donna il mondo chiama.
Come s'acquista onor, come Dio s'ama,
Com'è giunta onestà con leggiadria,
Ivi s'impara, e qual è dritta via
Di gir al Ciel, che lei aspetta e brama.
Ivi 'l parlar che nullo stile agguaglia,
E 'l bel tacere, e quei santi costumi
Ch'ingegno uman non può spiegar in carte.
L'infinita bellezza, ch'altrui abbaglia,
Non vi s'impara; ché quei dolci lumi
S'acquistan per ventura e non per arte.

(Sonnet 261)

IV

Doth any maiden seek the glorious fame
Of chastity, of strength, of courtesy?
Gaze in the eyes of that sweet enemy
Whom all the world doth as my lady name!
How honor grows, and pure devotion's flame,
How truth is joined with graceful dignity,
There thou mayst learn, and what the path may be
To that high heaven which doth her spirit claim;
There learn that speech, beyond all poet's skill,
And sacred silence, and those holy ways
Unutterable, untold by human heart.
But the infinite beauty that all eyes doth fill,
This none can learn! because its lovely rays
Are given by God's pure grace, and not by art.

V

O passi sparsi, o pensier vaghi e pronti,
O tenace memoria, o fero ardore,
O possente desire, o debil core,
O occhi miei, occhi non già, ma fonti;
O fronde, onor delle famose fronti,
O sola insegna al gemino valore;
O faticosa vita, o dolce errore,
Che mi fate ir cercando piagge e monti;
O bel viso, ov'Amor insieme pose
Gli sproni e 'l fren, ond'e' mi punge e volve
Com'a lui piace, e calcitrar non vale;
O anime gentili ed amorose,
S'alcuna ha 'l mondo; e voi nude ombre e polve;
Deh restate a veder qual è 'l mio male.

(Sonnet 161)

V

O wandering steps! O vague and busy dreams!
O changeless memory! O fierce desire!
O passion strong! heart weak with its own fire;
O eyes of mine! not eyes, but living streams;
O laurel boughs! whose lovely garland seems
The sole reward that glory's deeds require!
O haunted life! delusion sweet and dire,
That all my days from slothful rest redeems;
O beauteous face! where Love has treasured well
His whip and spur, the sluggish heart to move
At his least will; nor can it find relief.
O souls of love and passion! if ye dwell
Yet on this earth, and ye, great Shades of Love!
Linger, and see my passion and my grief.

VI

I' vidi in terra angelici costumi
E celesti bellezze al mondo sole;
Tal che di rimembrar mi giova e dole;
Ché quant'io miro par sogni, ombre e fumi.
E vidi lagrimar que' duo bei lumi,
C'han fatto mille volle invidia al Sole;
Ed udii sospirando dir parole
Che farian gir i monti e stare i fiumi.
Amor, senno, valor, pietate e doglia
Facean piangendo un più dolce concento
D'ogni altro che nel mondo udir si soglia:
Ed era 'l cielo all'armonia sì 'ntento,
Che non si vedea 'n ramo mover foglia;
Tanta dolcezza avea pien l'aere e 'l vento.

(Sonnet 156)

VI

I once beheld on earth celestial graces
And heavenly beauties scarce to mortals known,
Whose memory yields nor joy nor grief alone,
But all things else in cloud and dreams effaces.
I saw how tears had left their weary traces
Within those eyes that once the sun outshone,
I heard those lips, in low and plaintive moan,
Breathe words to stir the mountains from their places.
Love, wisdom, courage, tenderness, and truth
Made in their mourning strains more high and dear
Than ever wove soft sounds for mortal ear;
And heaven seemed listening in such saddest ruth
The very leaves upon the bough to soothe,
Such sweetness filled the blissful atmosphere.

VII

Gli occhi di ch'io parlai sì caldamente,
E le braccia e le mani e i piedi e 'l viso
Che m'avean sì da me stesso diviso
E fatto singular dall'altra gente;
Le crespe chiome d'or puro lucente,
E 'l lampeggiar dell'angelico riso
Che solean far in terra un paradiso,
Poca polvere son, che nulla sente.
Ed io pur vivo; onde mi doglio e sdegno,
Rimaso senza 'l lume ch'amai tanto,
In gran fortuna e 'n disarmato legno.
Or sia qui fine al mio amoroso canto:
Secca è la vena dell'usato ingegno,
E la cetera mia rivolta in pianto.

(Sonnet 292)

VII

Those eyes, 'neath which my passionate rapture rose,
The arms, hands, feet, the beauty that erewhile
Could my own soul from its own self beguile,
And in a separate world of dreams enclose,
The hair's bright tresses, full of golden glows,
And the soft lightning of the angelic smile
That changed this earth to some celestial isle, –
Are now but dust, poor dust, that nothing knows.
And yet I live! Myself I grieve and scorn,
Left dark without the light I loved in vain,
Adrift in tempest on a bark forlorn;
Dead is the source of all my amorous strain,
Dry is the channel of my thoughts outworn,
And my sad harp can sound but notes of pain.

VIII

Soleasi nel mio cor star bella e viva,
Com'alta donna in loco umile e basso:
Or son fatt'io per l'ultimo suo passo,
Non pur mortal ma morto; ed ella è diva.
L'alma d'ogni suo ben spogliata e priva,
Amor della sua luce ignudo e casso
Devrian della pietà romper un sasso:
Ma non è chi lor duol riconti o scriva;
Ché piangon dentro, ov'ogni orecchia è sorda,
Se non la mia, cui tanta doglia ingombra,
Ch'altro che sospirar, nulla m'avanza.
Veramente siam noi polvere ed ombra;
Veramente la voglia è cieca e 'ngorda;
Veramente fallace è la speranza.

(Sonnet 294)

VIII

She ruled in beauty o'er this heart of mine,
A noble lady in a humble home,
And now her time for heavenly bliss has come,
'Tis I am mortal proved, and she divine.
The soul that all its blessings must resign,
And love whose light no more on earth finds room
Might rend the rocks with pity for their doom,
Yet none their sorrows can in words enshrine;
They weep within my heart; no ears they find
Save mine alone, and I am crushed with care,
And naught remains to me save mournful breath.
Assuredly but dust and shade we are;
Assuredly desire is mad and blind;
Assuredly its hope but ends in death.

IX

Levommi il mio pensier in parte ov'era
Quella ch'io cerco e non ritrovo in terra:
Ivi, fra lor che 'l terzo cerchio serra,
La rividi più bella e meno altera.
Per man mi prese e disse: in questa spera
Sarai ancor meco, se 'l desir non erra;
I' son colei che ti die' tanta guerra,
E compie' mia giornata innanzi sera.
Mio ben non cape in intelletto umano:
Te solo aspetto, e, quel che tanto amasti,
E laggiuso è rimaso, il mio bel velo.
Deh perchè tacque ed allargò la mano?
Ch'al suon de' detti sì pietosi e casti
Poco mancò ch'io non rimasi in cielo.

(Sonnet 302)

IX

Dreams bore my fancy to that region where
She dwells whom here I seek, but cannot see.
'Mid those who in the loftiest heaven be
I looked on her, less haughty and more fair.
She took my hand, she said, "Within this sphere,
If hope deceive not, thou shalt dwell with me:
I filled thy life with war's wild agony;
Mine own day closed ere evening could appear.
My bliss no human thought can understand;
I wait for thee alone, and that fair veil
Of beauty thou dost love shall yet retain."
Why was she silent then, why dropped my hand
Ere those delicious tones could quite avail
To bid my mortal soul in heaven remain?

X

Dolci durezze e placide repulse,
Piene di casto amore e di pietate;
Leggiadri sdegni, che le mie infiammate
Voglie tempraro (or me n'accorgo) e 'nsulse;
Gentil parlar, in cui chiaro refulse
Con somma cortesia somma onestate;
Fior di virtù, fontana di beltate,
Ch'ogni basso pensier del cor m'avulse;
Divino sguardo, da far l'uom felice,
Or fiero in affrenar la mente ardita
A quel che giustamente si disdice,
Or presto a confortar mia frale vita;
Questo bel variar fu la radice
Di mia salute, che altramente era ita.

(Sonnet 351)

X

Gentle severity, repulses mild,
Full of chaste love and pity sorrowing;
Graceful rebukes, that had the power to bring
Back to itself a heart by dreams beguiled;
A tender voice, whose accents undefiled
Held sweet restraints, all duty honoring;
The bloom of virtue; purity's clear spring
To cleanse away base thoughts and passions wild;
Divinest eyes to make a lover's bliss,
Whether to bridle in the wayward mind
Lest its wild wanderings should the pathway miss,
Or else its griefs to soothe, its wounds to bind;
This sweet completeness of thy life it is
Which saved my soul; no other peace I find.

XI

Gli angeli eletti e l'anime beate
Cittadine del cielo, il primo giorno
Che Madonna passò, le fur intorno
Piene di maraviglia e di pietate.
Che luce è questa, e qual nova beltate?
Dicean tra lor; perch'abito sì adorno
Dal mondo errante a quest'alto soggiorno
Non salì mai in tutta questa etate.
Ella contenta aver cangiato albergo,
Si paragona pur coi più perfetti;
E parte ad or ad or si volge a tergo
Mirando s'io la seguo, e par ch'aspetti:
Ond'io voglie e pensier tutti al ciel ergo;
Perch'io l'odo pregar pur ch'i' m'affretti.

(Sonnet 346)

XI

The holy angels and the spirits blest,
Celestial bands, upon that day serene
When first my love went by in heavenly sheen,
Came thronging, wondering at the gracious guest.
"What light is here, in what new beauty drest?"
They said among themselves; "for none has seen
Within this age arrive so fair a mien
From changing earth unto immortal rest."
And she, contented with her new-found bliss,
Ranks with the perfect in that upper sphere,
Yet ever and anon looks back on this,
To watch for me, as if for me she stayed.
So strive my thoughts, lest that high heaven I miss.
I hear her call, and must not be delayed.

XII

Dicemi spesso il mio fidato speglio,
L'animo stanco e la cangiata scorza
E la scemata mia destrezza e forza;
Non ti nasconder più; tu se' pur veglio.
Obbedir a Natura in tutto è il meglio;
Ch'a contender con lei il tempo ne sforza.
Subito allor, com'acqua il foco ammorza,
D'un lungo e grave sonno mi risveglio:
E veggio ben che 'l nostro viver vola,
E ch'esser non si può più d'una volta;
E 'n mezzo 'l cor mi sona una parola
Di lei ch'è or dal suo bel nodo sciolta,
Ma ne' suoi giorni al mondo fu sì sola,
Ch'a tutte, s'i' non erro, fama ha tolta.

(Sonnet 361)

XII

Oft by my faithful mirror I am told,
And by my mind outworn and altered brow,
My earthly powers impaired and weakened now, –
"Deceive thyself no more, for thou art old!"
Who strives with Nature's laws is over-bold,
And Time to his commandment bids us bow.
Like fire that waves have quenched, I calmly vow
In life's long dream no more my sense to fold.
And while I think, our swift existence flies,
And none can live again earth's brief career, –
Then in my deepest heart the voice replies
Of one who now has left this mortal sphere,
But walked alone through earthly destinies,
And of all women is to fame most dear.

XIII

Vago augelletto che cantando vai,
Ovver piangendo il tuo tempo passato,
Vedendoti la notte e 'l verno a lato,
E 'l dì dopo le spalle e i mesi gai;
Se come i tuoi gravosi affanni sai,
Così sapessi il mio simile stato,
Verresti in grembo a questo sconsolato
A partir seco i dolorosi guai.
I' non so se le parti sarian pari;
Che quella cui tu piangi è forse in vita,
Di ch'a me Morte e 'l Ciel son tanto avari:
Ma la stagione e l'ora men gradita,
Col membrar de' dolci anni e degli amari,
A parlar teco con pietà m'invita.

(Sonnet 353)

XIII

Sweet wandering bird that singest on thy way,
Or mournest yet the time for ever past,
Watching night come and spring receding fast,
Day's bliss behind thee and the seasons gay, –
If thou my griefs against thine own couldst weigh,
Thou couldst not guess how long my sorrows last;
Yet thou mightst hide thee from the wintry blast
Within my breast, and thus my pains allay.
Yet may not all thy woes be named with mine,
Since she whom thou dost mourn may live, yet live,
But death and heaven still hold my spirit's bride;
And all those long past days of sad decline
With all the joys remembered years can give
Still bid me ask "Sweet bird! with me abide!"

XIV

La gola e 'l sonno e l'oziose piume
Hanno del mondo ogni vertù sbandita,
Ond'è dal corso suo quasi smarrita
Nostra natura, vinta dal costume;
Ed è sì spento ogni benigno lume
Del ciel, per cui s'informa umana vita,
Che per cosa mirabile s'addita
Chi vuol far d'Elicona nascer fiume.
Qual vaghezza di lauro? qual di mirto?
Povera e nuda vai, filosofia,
Dice la turba al vil guadagno intesa.
Pochi compagni avrai per l'altra via:
Tanto ti prego più, gentile spirto,
Non lassar la magnanima tua impresa.

(Sonnet 7)

XIV

Lust and dull slumber and the lazy hours
Have well nigh banished virtue from mankind.
Hence have man's nature and his treacherous mind
Left their free course, enmeshed in sin's soft bowers.
The very light of heaven hath lost its powers
Mid fading ways our loftiest dreams to find;
Men jeer at him whose footsteps are inclined
Where Helicon from dewy fountains showers.
Who seeks the laurel? who the myrtle twines?
"Wisdom, thou goest a beggar and unclad,"
So scoffs the crowd, intent on worthless gain.
Few are the hearts that prize the poet's lines:
Yet, friend, the more I hail thy spirit glad!
Let not the glory of thy purpose wane!

XV

Voi ch'ascoltate in rime sparse il suono
Di quei sospiri ond'io nudriva il core
In sul mio primo giovenile errore,
Quand' era in parte altr'uom da quel ch'i' sono;
Del vario stile, in ch'io piango e ragiono
Fra le vane speranze e 'l van dolore,
Ove sia chi per prova intenda amore,
Spero trovar pietà, non che perdono.
Ma ben veggi' or, sì come al popol tutto
Favola fui gran tempo: onde sovente
Di me medesmo meco mi vergogno:
E del mio vaneggiar vergogna è 'l frutto,
E 'l pentirsi, e 'l conoscer chiaramente
Che quanto piace al mondo è breve sogno.

(Sonnet 1)

XV

O ye who trace through scattered verse the sound
Of those long sighs wherewith I fed my heart
Amid youth's errors, when in greater part
That man unlike this present man was found;
For the mixed strain which here I do compound
Of empty hopes and pains that vainly start,
Whatever soul hath truly felt love's smart,
With pity and with pardon will abound.
But now I see full well how long I earned
All men's reproof; and oftentimes my soul
Lies crushed by its own grief; and it doth seem
For such misdeed shame is the fruitage whole,
And wild repentance and the knowledge learned
That worldly joy is still a short, short dream.

ILLUSTRATIONS

Portraits of Francesco Petrarch
(this page and over)

DOMINVS FRANCISCVS PETRARCHA

Giorgio Vasari, Six Tuscan Poets, 1544, Minneapolis

Boccaccio, Vision of Petrarch, 1467, Glasgow

MS 1954 Petrarch: Epistolae seniles. Italy, late 14th c.

Francesco Petrarch, a page from his letters, 14th century

Francesco Petrarch
by Justo de Gante,
15th century (left).

Laura de Sade

Josef Manes, Laura and Petrarch, 1845

Philippe-Jacques van Breé, Laure et Pétrarque à Fontaine de Vaucluse

Petrarch and Laura,
anonymous artist,
19th century (above).
Nicaise de Keyser,
Petrarch and Laura,
1842 (left).

A NOTE ON
FRANCESCO PETRARCH

By Cassidy Hughes

Francesco Petrarch (Francesco Petrarca, 1304-1374) is the supreme poet of love in the Western tradition, alongside poets such as Sappho and William Shakespeare. Francesco Petrarch is also the Renaissance artist and humanist *par excellence*. Petrarchism is termed the longest poetic tradition in the Occident, and Petrarch has influenced poets such as Maurice Scève, Sir Thomas Wyatt, Torquato Tasso, Edmund Spenser, Michael Drayton, Joachim Du Bellay, Pierre de Ronsard, Rainer Maria Rilke and Robert Graves, among hundreds of others.

Francesco Petrarch is also called the first modernist: his poetic persona is an early modern version of one of those now familiar alienated, bourgeois, modern outsiders, the kind found in the work of Jean-Paul Sartre, Knut Hamsun, André Gide, Albert Camus and Arthur Rimbaud.

Francesco Petrarch is a poet's poet, an artist who tried to make art in the purest fashion, who burned brightly for his art. He is one of the first poets to exalt the individual in the way we recognize as modern, and Petrarch's ruthless self-analysis seems wholly in tune with that of, say, Arthur Rimbaud, Julia Kristeva,

Paul Valéry, Lawrence Durrell or Virginia Woolf.

But it is as a love poet that Francesco Petrarch is celebrated – as a love poet rather than a rhetorician, humanist or philosopher (although his work in those areas is very important). Petrarch's *Canzoniere*, often also known as the *Rime Sparse*, lies at the heart of his achievement: it comprises 366 poems about love, written in Italian and worked on right up until Petrarch's death in 1374. In the *Canzoniere*, there are hundreds of sonnets, 29 *canzoni*, 7 *ballate*, 9 *sestine* and 4 *madrigali*. Petrarch's other major works included *Secretum, Triumphs, Africa, De Vita Solitaria*, verse epistles, biographies, allegorical ecologues and hundreds of letters.

Love rules, and Francesco Petrarch is so popular partly because of his love poetry, because he writes so well about love, because he flatters the reader's received notions of love, because most critics (the people who exalt Petrarch in critical writings) are male, and Petrarch's philosophy of love is masculinist and patriarchal. Petrarch celebrates mainly masculine ideas of love, sex, seduction and romance. He trades on desire, and desire is at the heart of Western culture (in movies, pop songs, advertizing, novels, magazines, radio shows, TV sit corms, fashion, etc). The desire is for the unattainable – variously imagined to be the distant but beautiful woman, the Holy Grail, ideal love, heaven, world peace, no poverty, etc.

The focus of the quest in Francesco Petrarch's *Rime Sparse* is Laura de Sade, the beloved woman (she was probably Laura de Noves, wife of the Count Hugues de Sade. As modern comment-ators can't resist pointing out, Laura's husband was an ancestor of the Marquis de Sade, further embedding Petrarch in the *avant garde* and progressive literary tradition of Europe).

Francesco Petrarch emerges as the poet who is the apotheosis of courtly love, and his *Canzoniere* is the supreme example of the troubadour ethic. At the same time, the *Rime Sparse* is a decadent text, falling into self-parody and too sweetly refined artifice. The power of Petrarch's work is even so undeniable. Articles and magazines and quarterlies and journals abound which deal with

Petrarch and aspects of his poetry, philosophy and rhetoric (including: *Convivium, Journal of the History of Ideas, Modern Language Notes, Studies in Philology. Giornala storico del la letteratura itallana, Pacific Coast Philology, Italian Philological Quarterly, Cultura Neolatina, Forum Italicum, Dante Studies, Yearbook of Italian Studies, Lettere Italiane, Italian Quarterly, Italianistica, Italia medioevale et umanistica, Enciclopedia Dantesca, Diacritics, Journal of Medieval and Renaissance Studies, Romance Notes* and *Renaissance and Reformation*).

BIBLIOGRAPHY

FRANCESCO PETRARCH

F. Petrarch. *Petrarch's Lyric Poems; the Rime Sparse and other Lyrics*, tr. Robert M. Durling, Harvard University Pr4ess, Cambridge, MA, 1978

Petrarch and Petrarchism, tr. Stephen Minta, Manchester University Press, Manchester, 1980

Selected Poems, ed. T. Gwynfor Griffith & P.R.J. Hainsworth, Manchester University Press, Manchester, 1971

Selected Poems, tr. Anthony Mortimer, University of Alabama Press, Alabama, 1977

Selections From the 'Canonziere' and Other Works, tr. Mark Musa, Oxford University Press, Oxford, 1985

ON PETRARCH

T. Bahti. "Petrarch and the Scene of Writing: A Reading of *Rime* CXXIX", *Yale Italian Studies*, 1, 1980

– . *Ends of the Lyric: Direction and Consequence in Western Poetry*, Johns Hopkins University Press, Baltimore, MD, 1996

T. Barolini. "The Making of a Lyric Sequence: Time and Narrative in Petrarch's *Rerum vulgarium fragmenta*", *Modern Language Notes*, 104, 1989

A. Bernardo, ed. *Francesco Petrarca*, Albany, NY, 1980

– . "The importance of the non-love poems in Petrarch's *Cazoniere*", *Italica*, 27, 1950

– . "Petrarch's attitude towards Dante", *Proceedings of the Modern Language Association*, 70, 1955

– . "Petrarch and the Art of Literature", in Molinaro, 1973

– . *Petrarch, Laura, and the 'Triumphs'*, Albany, NY, 1974

– . & A.L. Pellegrini, eds. *Dante, Petrarch, Boccaccio, Medieval and Renaissance Texts and Studies*, Binghamton, 1983

E. Bigi. "La rima del Petrarca", *Studi petrarcheschi*, 7, 1961

− . "La ballate del Petrarca", *Giornale storico della letteratura italiana*, 151, 1974

− . "Alcuni aspetti dello stile del *Canzoniere* petrarchesco", *Dal Petrarca al Leopardi*, Milan, 1954

M. Bishop. *Petrarch and His World*, Indiana University Press Bloomington, London, 1963

E.L. Boggs. "Cino and Petrarca", *Modern Language Notes*, 94, 1979

U. Bosc. *Francesco Petrarca*, Bari, 1961

M. O'Rouke Boyle. *Petrarch's Genius: Pentimento and Prophecy*, University of California Press, Berkeley, CA, 1991

G. Braden. "Love and Fame: The Petrarchan Career", in Smith, 1986

J. Brenkman. "Writing, Desire, Dialectic in Petrarch's *Rime 23*", *Pacific Coast Philology*, 9, 1974

G.A. Cesareo. *Su le 'poesie volgari' del Petrarca*, Rocca San Casciano, 1898

E. Chiappelli. *Studi sui linguaggio del Petrarca: la canzone della visioni*, Florence, 1971

G. Cipolla. "Labyrinthine Imagery in Petrarch", *Italica*, 54, 1977

R.J. Clements. "Préhistoire de l'aura de Pétraque", in *Varianti e altra linguistica*, 193-9, Einaudi, Turin, 1970

G. Contini. "Anti-Petrarchism of the Pléiade", *Modern Philology*, 39, 1942

Convegno Internazionale Francesco Petrarca, Rome, 1976

K. Cool. "The Petrarchan Landscape as Palimpsest", *Journal of Medieval and Renaissance Studies*, 11, 1981

M. Cottino-Jones. "The Myth of Apollo and Daphne in Petrarch's *Canzoniere*", in Scaglione, 1975

D. Dtuschke. "The Anniversary Poems in Petrarch's *Canzoniere*", *Italica*, 58, 1981

− . *Francesco Petrarca: Canzone XXIII From First to Final Version*, Ravenna, 1977

R.M. Durling. "Petrarch's 'Giovene donna sotto un verde lauro'", *Modern Language Notes*, 86, 1971

L. Enterline. "Embodied Voices: Petrarch Reading (Himself Reading) Ovid", in Finucci, 1994

F. Figurelli. "L'architettura del sonetto in Francesco Petrarca", *Studi petrarcheschi*, 7, 1961

K. Foster. *Petrarch: Poet and Humanist*, Edinburgh, 1984

J. Freccero. "The Fig Tree and the Laurel: Petrarch's Poetics", *Diacritics*, Spring, 1975

G. Genot. "Petrarque et la scene du regard", *Journal of Medieval and Renaissance Studies*, 2, 1972

E. Gianturco. "The Double Gift: Inner Vision and Pictorial Sense in Petrarch", *Renaissance and Reformation*, 8, 1972

P. Hainsworth. *Petrarch the Poet: An Introduction to the 'Rerum Vulgarium*

Fragmente', Routledge, London, 1988

F.J. Jones. "Laura's date of birth and the calendrical system implicit in the *Canzoniere*", *Italianistica*, 1, 1983

– . "Arguments in favour of a calendrical structure for Petrarch's *Canzoniere*", *Modern Language Review*, 79, 1984

– . "Further evidence of the identity of Petrarch's Laura", *Italian Studies*, 39, 1984

H.A. Mathes. "Petrarch's Tranquillo Porto'", *Italica*, 26, 1949

W.J. Kennedy. "Petrarchan Textuality", in Brownlee, 1989

G. Mazzotta. "Petrarch's Song 126", in Caws, 1986

– . "The *Canzoniere* and the Language of the Self", *Studies in Philology*, 75, 1978

– . ed. *The World of Petrarch*, Duke University Press, Durham, NC, 1993

M. Perugi. *Trovatori a Valchiusa: un frammento della cultura provenzale del Petrarca*, Studi sul Petrarca, 18, Antenore, Padua, 1985

J. Petrie. *Petrarch*: P. Possiedi: "Petrarca Petrosco", *Forum italicum*, 8, 1974

A.E. Quaglio. *Francesco Petrarca*, Milan, 1967

M.S. Regan. "Petrarch's Courtly and Christian Vocabularies: Language in *Canzoniere* 61-63", *Romance Notes*, 15, 1974

F. Rigolot. "Nature and Function of Paronomasia in the *Canzoniere*", *Italian Quarterly*, 18, 1974

T. Roche. "The Calendrical Structure of Petrarch's *Canzoniere*", *Studies in Philology*, 7, 1974

– . *Petrarch and the English Sonnet Sequences*, AMS Press, New York, 1989

N. Rosenberg. "Petrarch's Limping: The Foot Unequal to the Eye", *Modern Language Notes*, 77, 1962

I. Scarano, ed. *Francesco Petrarca*, Naples, 1972

F. Schalk, ed. *Petrarca 1304-1374: Beitrage zu Werk und Wirkung*, Frankfurt, 1975

M. Shapiro. *Hieroglyph of Time: The Petrarchan Sestina*, Minneapolis, MN, 1980

B.T. Sozzi. *Petrarca*, Palermo, 1963

S. Sturm-Maddox. "Petrarch's Serpent in the Grass: The Fall as Subtext in the *Rime Sparse*", *Journal of Medieval and Renaissance Studies*, 13, 1983

– . "Petrarch's Siren", *Italian Quarterly*, 103, 1986

J. Tilden. "Spiritual Conflict in Petrarch's *Canzoniere*", in F. Schalk

M. Turchi. "Il centenario del Petrarca e la critica", *Italianistica*, 7, 1978

G. Velli. "La memoria poetica del Petrarca", *Italia medievale e umanistica*, 19, 1976

– . "La metafora del Petrarca", in Goldin, 1980

M. Waller. *Petrarch's Poetics and Literary History*, Amherst, MA, 1980

E.H. Wilkins. *Petrarch at Vaucluse*, Chicago University Press, Chicago, IL, 1958

– . *The Making of the 'Canzoniere' and other Petrarchan Studies*, Rome, 1951

– . *Life of Petrarch*, Chicago University Press, Chicago, IL, 1961
– . *Studies in the Life and Works of Petrarch*, Harvard University Press, Cambridge, MA, 1955
– . *Petrarch's Eight Years in Milan*, Harvard University Press, Cambridge, MA, 1958
– . *Petrarch's Later Years*, Harvard University Press, Cambridge, MA, 1959
– . *Petrarch's Correspondence*, Harvard University Press, Cambridge, MA, 1960
E. Williamson. "A Consideration of 'Virgine bella'", *Italica*, 29, 1952

Life, Life
Selected Poems

Arseny Tarkovsky

translated and edited by Virginia Rounding

Arseny Tarkovsky is the neglected Russian poet, father of the acclaimed film director
Andrei Tarkovsky. This new book gathers together many of Tarkovsky's most lyrical
and heartfelt poems, in Rounding's clear, new translations. Many of Tarkovsky's poems
appeared in his son's films, such as *Mirror, Stalker, Nostalghia and The Sacrifice*.
There is an introduction by Rounding, and a bibliography of both Arseny and
Andrei Tarkovsky.

Bibliography and notes 124pp 3rd ed ISBN 9781861712660 Hbk ISBN 9781861711144

MAURICE SENDAK

& the art of children's book illustration

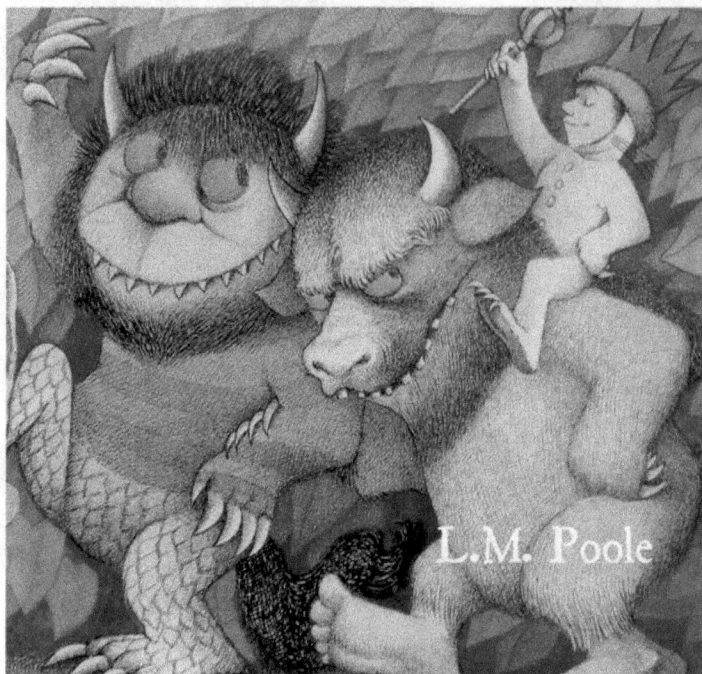

L.M. Poole

Maurice Sendak is the widely acclaimed American children's book author and illustrator. This critical study focuses on his famous trilogy, *Where the Wild Things Are*, *In the Night Kitchen* and *Outside Over There*, as well as the early works and Sendak's superb depictions of the Grimm Brothers' fairy tales in *The Juniper Tree*. L.M. Poole begins with a chapter on children's book illustration, in particular the treatment of fairy tales. Sendak's work is situated within the history of children's book illustration, and he is compared with many contemporary authors.

Fully illustrated. The book has been revised and updated for this edition.
ISBN 9781861714282 Pbk   ISBN 9781861713469 Hbk

In the Dim Void

Samuel Beckett's Late Trilogy: *Company, Ill Seen, Ill Said* and *Worstward Ho*

by Gregory Johns

This book discusses the luminous beauty and dense, rigorous poetry of Samuel Beckett's late works, *Company, Ill Seen, Ill Said* and *Worstward Ho*. Gregory Johns looks back over Beckett's long writing career, charting the development from the *Molloy-Malone Dies-Unnamable* trilogy through the 'fizzles' of the 1960s to the elegiac lyricism of the *Company* series. Johns compares the trilogy with late plays such as *Ghosts, Footfalls* and *Rockaby*.

Bibliography, notes. Illustrated. 120pp
ISBN 9781861712974 Pbk and ISBN 9781861712608 Hbk
9781861713407 E-book

Beauties, Beasts, and Enchantment

CLASSIC FRENCH FAIRY TALES

Translated and with an Introduction
by Jack Zipes

A collection of 36 classic French fairy tales translated by renowned writer Jack Zipes.
Cinderella, Beauty and the Beast, Sleeping Beauty and *Little Red Riding Hood* are among the
classic fairy tales in this amazing book.
Includes illustrations from fairy tale collections.
Jack Zipes has written and published widely on fairy tales.

'Terrific... a succulent array of 17th and 18th century 'salon' fairy tales'
- *The New York Times Book Review*

'These tales are adventurous, thrilling in a way fairy tales are meant to be... The translation
from the French is modern, happily free of archaic and hyperbolic language... a fine and
sophisticated collection' - *New York Tribune*

'Enjoyable to read... a unique collection of French regional folklore' - *Library Journal*

'Charming stories accompanied by attractive pen-and-ink drawings' - *Chattanooga Times*

Introduction and illustrations   612pp.   ISBN 9781861712510 Pbk   ISBN 9781861713193 Hbk

CRESCENT MOON PUBLISHING

web: www.crmoon.com e-mail: cresmopub@yahoo.co.uk

ARTS, PAINTING, SCULPTURE

The Art of Andy Goldsworthy
Andy Goldsworthy: Touching Nature
Andy Goldsworthy in Close-Up
Andy Goldsworthy: Pocket Guide
Andy Goldsworthy In America
Land Art: A Complete Guide
The Art of Richard Long
Richard Long: Pocket Guide
Land Art In the UK
Land Art in Close-Up
Land Art In the U.S.A.
Land Art: Pocket Guide
Installation Art in Close-Up
Minimal Art and Artists In the 1960s and After
Colourfield Painting
Land Art DVD, TV documentary
Andy Goldsworthy DVD, TV documentary
The Erotic Object: Sexuality in Sculpture From Prehistory to the Present Day
Sex in Art: Pornography and Pleasure in Painting and Sculpture
Postwar Art
Sacred Gardens: The Garden in Myth, Religion and Art
Glorification: Religious Abstraction in Renaissance and 20th Century Art
Early Netherlandish Painting
Leonardo da Vinci
Piero della Francesca
Giovanni Bellini
Fra Angelico: Art and Religion in the Renaissance
Mark Rothko: The Art of Transcendence
Frank Stella: American Abstract Artist
Jasper Johns
Brice Marden
Alison Wilding: The Embrace of Sculpture
Vincent van Gogh: Visionary Landscapes
Eric Gill: Nuptials of God
Constantin Brancusi: Sculpting the Essence of Things
Max Beckmann
Caravaggio
Gustave Moreau
Egon Schiele: Sex and Death In Purple Stockings
Delizioso Fotografico Fervore: Works In Process 1
Sacro Cuore: Works In Process 2
The Light Eternal: J.M.W. Turner
The Madonna Glorified: Karen Arthurs

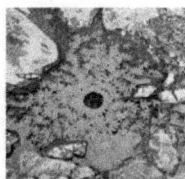

J.R.R. Tolkien: The Books, The Films, The Whole Cultural Phenomenon
J.R.R. Tolkien: Pocket Guide
Tolkien's Heroic Quest
The *Earthsea* Books of Ursula Le Guin
Beauties, Beasts and Enchantment: Classic French Fairy Tales
German Popular Stories by the Brothers Grimm
Philip Pullman and *His Dark Materials*
Sexing Hardy: Thomas Hardy and Feminism
Thomas Hardy's *Tess of the d'Urbervilles*
Thomas Hardy's *Jude the Obscure*
Thomas Hardy: The Tragic Novels
Love and Tragedy: Thomas Hardy
The Poetry of Landscape in Hardy

Wessex Revisited: Thomas Hardy and John Cowper Powys
Wolfgang Iser: Essays and Interviews
Petrarch, Dante and the Troubadours
Maurice Sendak and the Art of Children's Book Illustration
Andrea Dworkin

Cixous, Irigaray, Kristeva: The *Jouissance* of French Feminism
Julia Kristeva: Art, Love, Melancholy, Philosophy, Semiotics and Psychoanalysis
Hélène Cixous I Love You: The *Jouissance* of Writing
Luce Irigaray: Lips, Kissing, and the Politics of Sexual Difference
Peter Redgrove: Here Comes the Flood
Peter Redgrove: Sex-Magic-Poetry-Cornwall

Lawrence Durrell: Between Love and Death, East and West
Love, Culture & Poetry: Lawrence Durrell
Cavafy: Anatomy of a Soul
German Romantic Poetry: Goethe, Novalis, Heine, Hölderlin
Feminism and Shakespeare
Shakespeare: Love, Poetry & Magic

The Passion of D.H. Lawrence
D.H. Lawrence: Symbolic Landscapes
D.H. Lawrence: Infinite Sensual Violence
Rimbaud: Arthur Rimbaud and the Magic of Poetry
The Ecstasies of John Cowper Powys

Sensualism and Mythology: The Wessex Novels of John Cowper Powys
Amorous Life: John Cowper Powys and the Manifestation of Affectivity (H.W. Fawkner)
Postmodern Powys: New Essays on John Cowper Powys (Joe Boulter)
Rethinking Powys: Critical Essays on John Cowper Powys
Paul Bowles & Bernardo Bertolucci
Rainer Maria Rilke
Joseph Conrad: *Heart of Darkness*
In the Dim Void: Samuel Beckett
Samuel Beckett Goes into the Silence
André Gide: Fiction and Fervour
Jackie Collins and the Blockbuster Novel

Blinded By Her Light: The Love-Poetry of Robert Graves
The Passion of Colours: Travels In Mediterranean Lands
Poetic Forms

POETRY

Ursula Le Guin: Walking In Cornwall
Peter Redgrove: Here Comes The Flood
Peter Redgrove: Sex-Magic-Poetry-Cornwall
Dante: Selections From the Vita Nuova
Petrarch, Dante and the Troubadours
William Shakespeare: Sonnets
William Shakespeare: Complete Poems
Blinded By Her Light: The Love-Poetry of Robert Graves
Emily Dickinson: Selected Poems
Emily Brontë: Poems
Thomas Hardy: Selected Poems
Percy Bysshe Shelley: Poems
John Keats: Selected Poems
Joh n Keats: Poems of 1820
D.H. Lawrence: Selected Poems
Edmund Spenser: Poems
Edmund Spenser: Amoretti
John Donne: Poems
Henry Vaughan: Poems
Sir Thomas Wyatt: Poems
Robert Herrick: Selected Poems
Rilke: Space, Essence and Angels in the Poetry of Rainer Maria Rilke
Rainer Maria Rilke: Selected Poems
Friedrich Hölderlin: Selected Poems
Arseny Tarkovsky: Selected Poems
Arthur Rimbaud: Selected Poems
Arthur Rimbaud: A Season in Hell
Arthur Rimbaud and the Magic of Poetry
Novalis: Hymns To the Night
German Romantic Poetry
Paul Verlaine: Selected Poems
Elizaethan Sonnet Cycles
D.J. Enright: By-Blows
Jeremy Reed: Brigitte's Blue Heart
Jeremy Reed: Claudia Schiffer's Red Shoes
Gorgeous Little Orpheus
Radiance: New Poems
Crescent Moon Book of Nature Poetry
Crescent Moon Book of Love Poetry
Crescent Moon Book of Mystical Poetry
Crescent Moon Book of Elizabethan Love Poetry
Crescent Moon Book of Metaphysical Poetry
Crescent Moon Book of Romantic Poetry
Pagan America: New American Poetry

MEDIA, CINEMA, FEMINISM and CULTURAL STUDIES

J.R.R. Tolkien: The Books, The Films, The Whole Cultural Phenomenon
J.R.R. Tolkien: Pocket Guide
The *Lord of the Rings* Movies: Pocket Guide
The Cinema of Hayao Miyazaki
Hayao Miyazaki: *Princess Mononoke*: Pocket Movie Guide
Hayao Miyazaki: *Spirited Away*: Pocket Movie Guide
Tim Burton : Hallowe'en For Hollywood
Ken Russell
Ken Russell: *Tommy*: Pocket Movie Guide
The Ghost Dance: The Origins of Religion
The Peyote Cult
Cixous, Irigaray, Kristeva: The *Jouissance* of French Feminism
Julia Kristeva: Art, Love, Melancholy, Philosophy, Semiotics and Psychoanalysis
Luce Irigaray: Lips, Kissing, and the Politics of Sexual Difference
Hélene Cixous I Love You: The *Jouissance* of Writing
Andrea Dworkin
'Cosmo Woman': The World of Women's Magazines
Women in Pop Music
HomeGround: The Kate Bush Anthology
Discovering the Goddess (Geoffrey Ashe)
The Poetry of Cinema
The Sacred Cinema of Andrei Tarkovsky
Andrei Tarkovsky: Pocket Guide
Andrei Tarkovsky: *Mirror*: Pocket Movie Guide
Andrei Tarkovsky: *The Sacrifice*: Pocket Movie Guide
Walerian Borowczyk: Cinema of Erotic Dreams
Jean-Luc Godard: The Passion of Cinema
Jean-Luc Godard: *Hail Mary*: Pocket Movie Guide
Jean-Luc Godard: *Contempt*: Pocket Movie Guide
Jean-Luc Godard: *Pierrot le Fou*: Pocket Movie Guide
John Hughes and Eighties Cinema
Ferris Bueller's Day Off: Pocket Movie Guide
Jean-Luc Godard: Pocket Guide
The Cinema of Richard Linklater
Liv Tyler: Star In Ascendance
Blade Runner and the Films of Philip K. Dick
Paul Bowles and Bernardo Bertolucci
Media Hell: Radio, TV and the Press
An Open Letter to the BBC
Detonation Britain: Nuclear War in the UK
Feminism and Shakespeare
Wild Zones: Pornography, Art and Feminism
Sex in Art: Pornography and Pleasure in Painting and Sculpture
Sexing Hardy: Thomas Hardy and Feminism

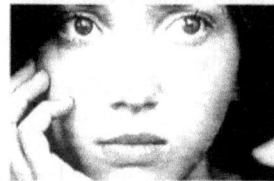

The Light Eternal is a model monograph, an exemplary job. The subject matter of the book is beautifully
organised and dead on beam. (Lawrence Durrell)
It is amazing for me to see my work treated with such passion and respect. (Andrea Dworkin)

CRESCENT MOON PUBLISHING
P.O. Box 1312, Maidstone, Kent, ME14 5XU, Great Britain. www.crmoon.com

cresmopub@yahoo.co.uk   www.crescentmoon.org.uk

www.ingramcontent.com/pod-product-compliance
Lightning Source LLC
Chambersburg PA
CBHW072046040426
42447CB00012BB/3040